Wild Animals Jungle Coloring Book

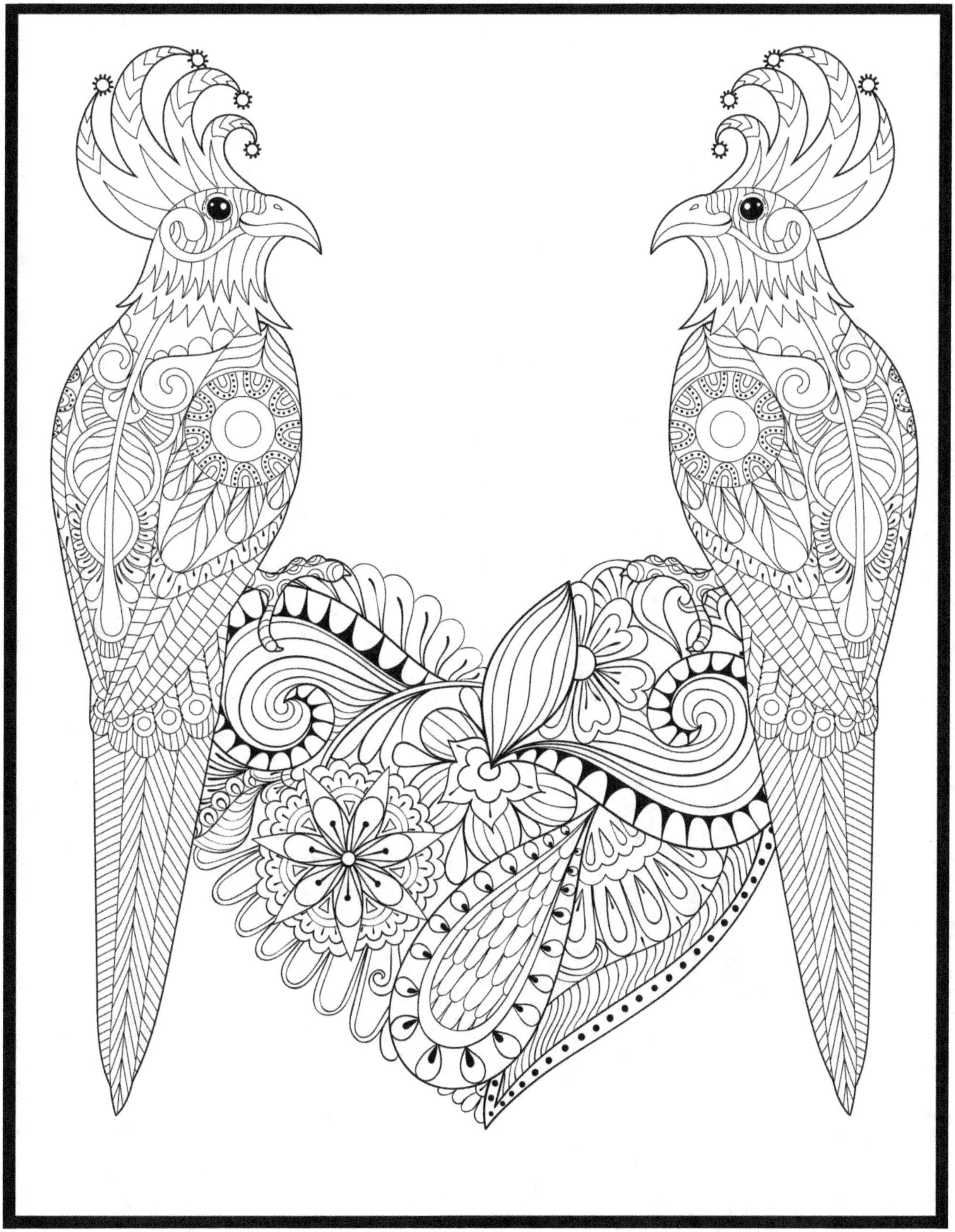

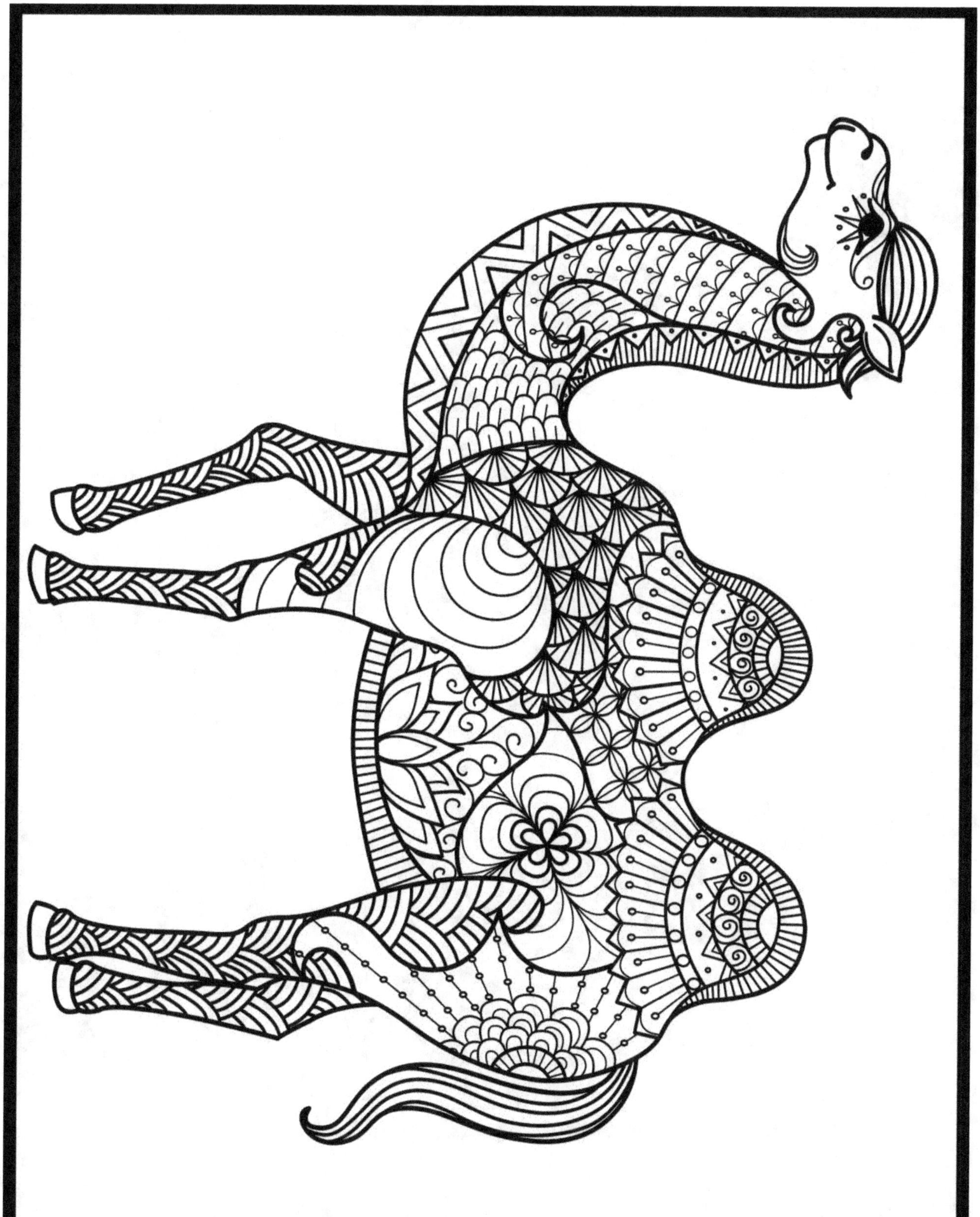

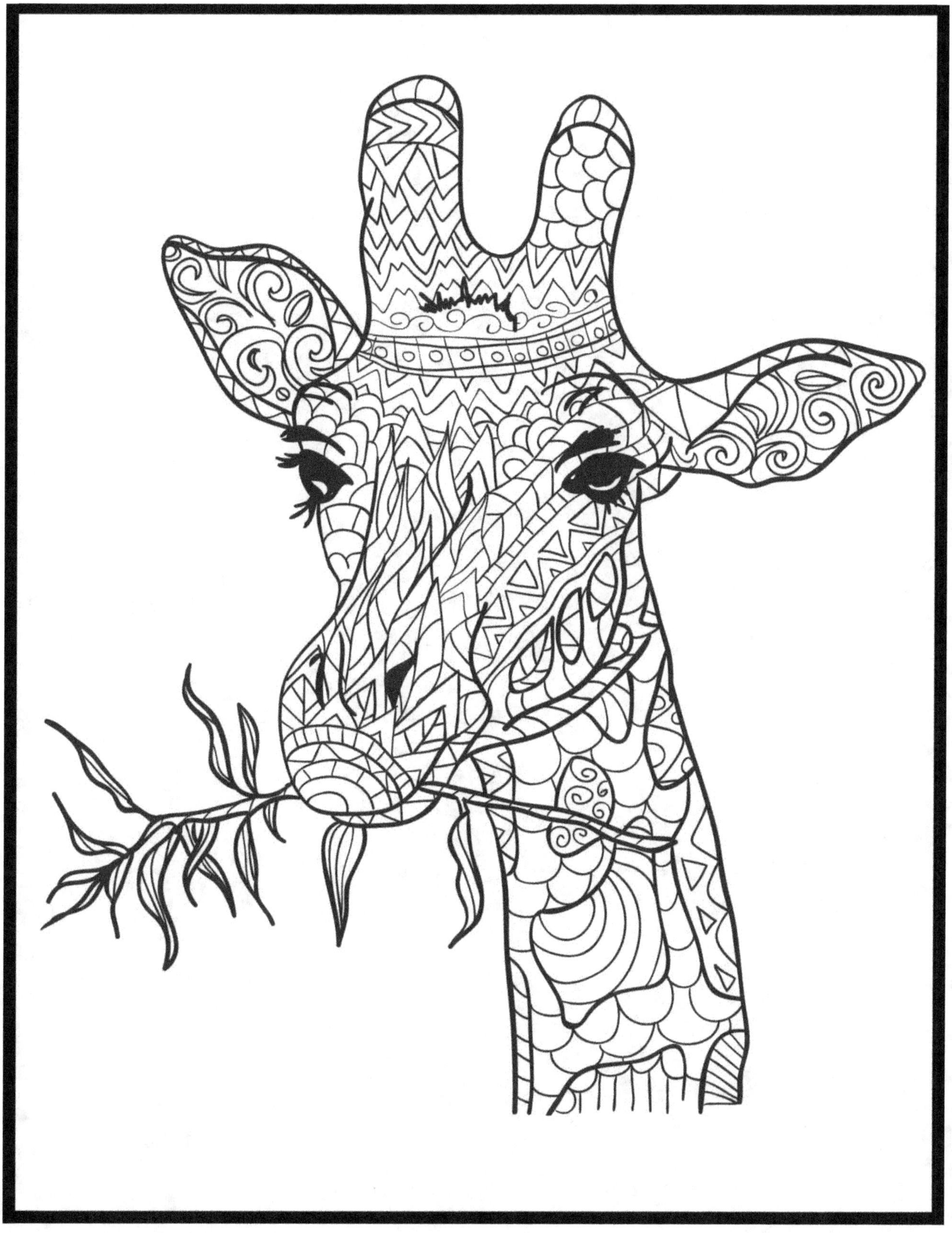

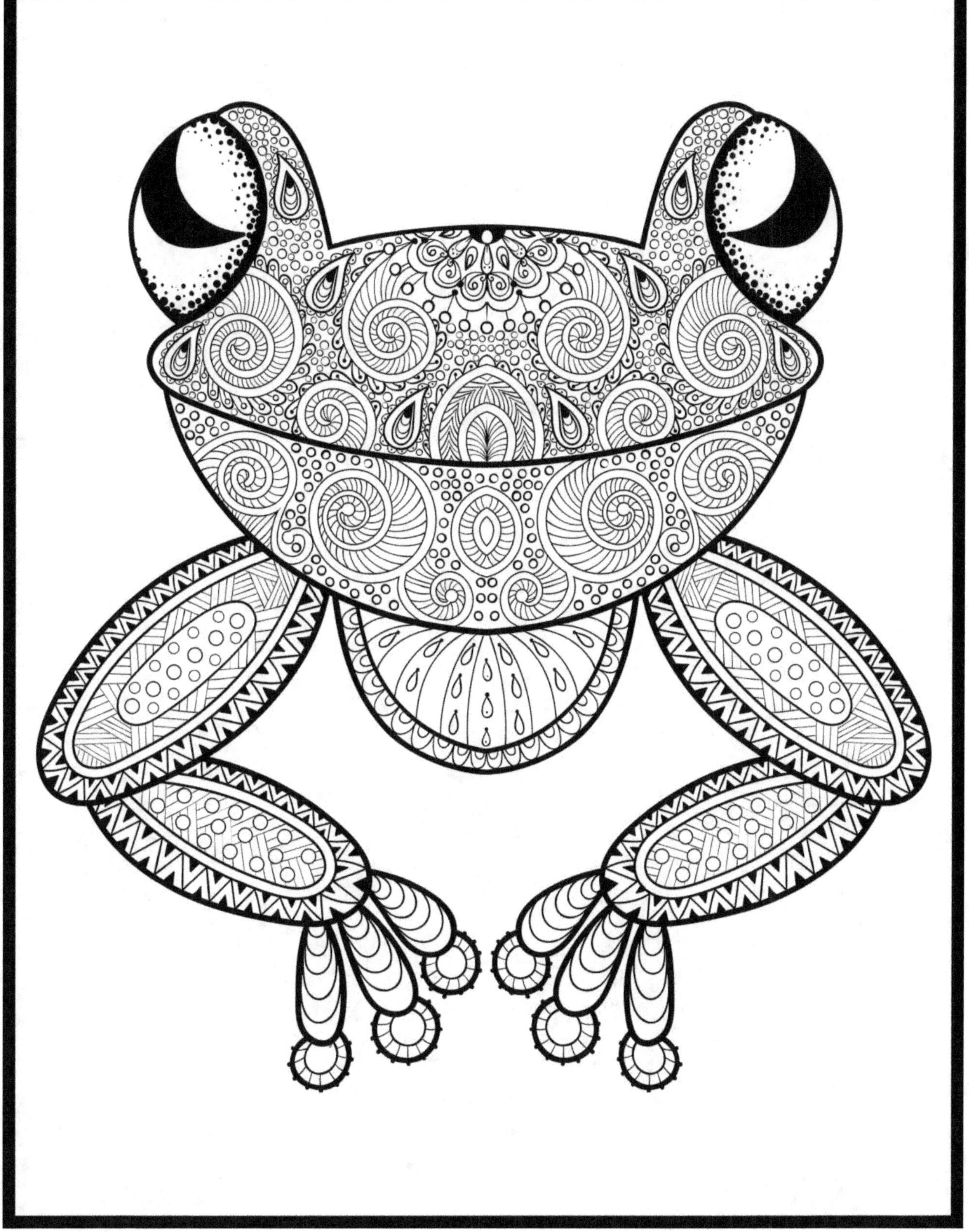

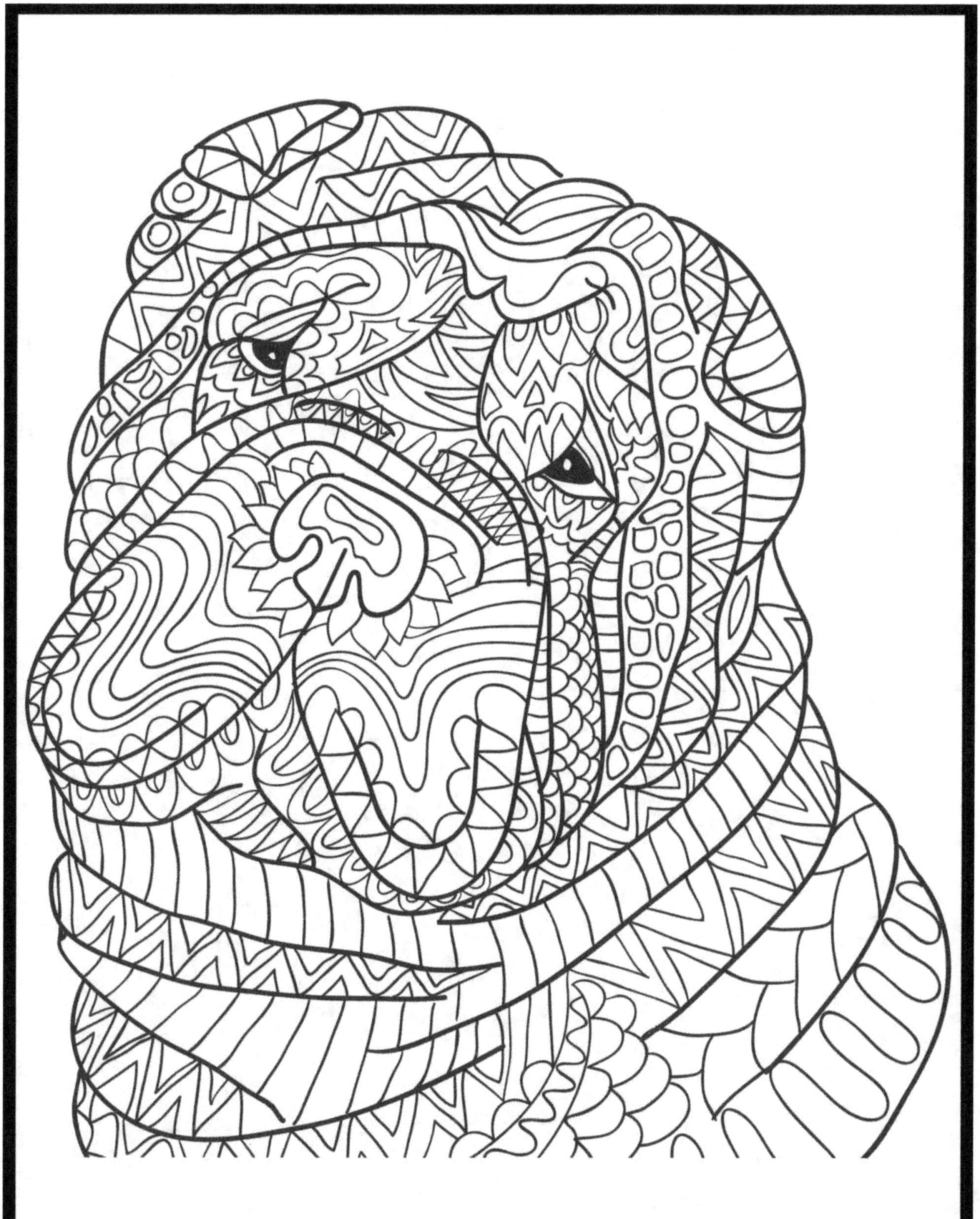

www.ingramcontent.com/pod-product-compliance
Lightning Source LLC
Chambersburg PA
CBHW081604220526
45468CB00010B/2765
9781721903139